THIS BOOK BELONGS TO

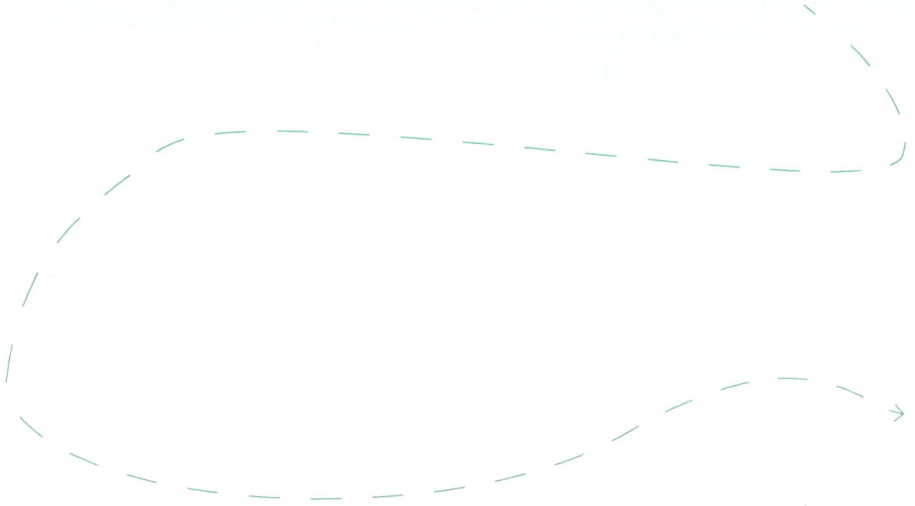

The ALPHABUGS

by Jeryl Christmas

Illustrated by Genevieve Stotler

A stands for Andy, a poor, lonely bug.
He lived all alone on a polka dot rug.
He wanted a friend, but who could it be?
Turn the page over, and then you will see.

Brucey joined Andy, but what a big bug!
There might not be room
for them both on the rug,
But Andy was happy—no longer alone.
Bruce was a friend he could call his own.

Clarence came next, walking in like a king
With his head held back,
while Bruce started to sing.
"Quiet!" yelled Clarence,
"I'll have none of that!"
He ordered them bring him a chair,
and he sat.

Danny came later, and oh, was he fat.
He munched on the chair
where Clarence now sat.
He munched and he crunched
'til the chair fell in two,
And Clarence fell down
with a great big to-do.

Edward was next to come into the crowd.
Standing perfectly straight,
he looked rather proud.
Not a word did he speak to one single bug.
He walked up beside them
and gave them a shrug.

Flora trailed close behind Edward, her kin.
The bugs gave a whistle like typical men.
But Edward raged at them.
Each feared for his life.
What the bugs didn't know was
that this was his wife.

Galloping Gill raced in like a flash.
He ran as if in the fifty-yard dash.
He screeched to a halt
and gazed at this crew.
The bugs turned their heads
and looked at him too.

Harvey marched in
like a prancing Great Dane.
He looked at young Flora,
but she was too plain.
"Just wait 'til they see my cute sister, Irene.
She's the best-looking bug
that you've ever seen."

Irene looked at no one as she strutted in.
(If you look at her sideways,
you'll see she's Harv's kin.)
She put on a show, dancing round for a bit,
Then ended her act by doing the split.

Jackson slid in with his arms
stretched out wide.
He was eager to speak and finally cried,
"Look out! Here she comes!
Oh, now it's too late!"
For in walked the well-known
and bossy bug, Kate.

Kate shook her finger at everyone there.
She talked very fiercely
and gave them a scare.
She said that her rules
and demands must be met,
And she would bring order to all of them yet.

Leo knew someone
who'd really bring peace
And announced the arrival
of mighty Maurice.
So Kate's job was threatened—
she'd have to step down,
For in walked Maurice,
complete with his crown.

Mighty Maurice was now their new king,
The top bug around, so they started to sing,
"Hail to our King! We're glad that he's here!"
And finished their song
with a loud, ringing cheer.

Ned inched his way to the midst of the ring.
He came to observe this talked-about king.
Ned was the oldest of all of them there.
To find a bug wiser would be very rare.

Oz was a round bug and as he rolled in,
On the upside-down turn,
he must tuck his chin.
This was a bug that met all with a grin.
He rolled over and over again and again.

Penny flew in on her beautiful wings,
But no one came near her
for fierce were her stings.
Penny was sad that they all stayed away,
For she had no friends
with whom she could play.

Queeny, a tidy bug, slowly walked in
And sniffed at the dirt—she was neat as a pin.
She yelled, "Come on, bugs.
Let's clean up this place!"
So each started scrubbing as if in a race.

Ramona came in to give her advice
And said that this place could never look nice.
She cried, "There are too many living in here!"
But Bruce yelled, "Not so!"
which brought on a cheer.

Slithering Sam slid into the room
And climbed to the top
of old Queeny's broom.
He yelled, "Listen here!" to all of the bugs.
"This place would look neat
if you'd bring in more rugs."

Tate was the first to supply his own rug.
He thought there should be
one for every bug.
He laid his on top of the polka dot one
And thought it looked great—
so now for some fun.

Uncle Uriah edged into the crowd
And said, "Y'all have fun,
but don't be too loud.
I'm well overdue for a long, restful nap,
And I'll go just as soon as I find my nightcap."

Vince was the next one to finally appear.
Just four bugs to go
and they all would be here.
He saw twenty-six after counting the rest,
Same as the alphabet—Who would have
guessed?

Will walked in with a smile on his face,
So glad he had made it to stand in his place.
But no one was lined up.
Where was the show?
The bugs yelled to Will,
"There are three more to go!"

Xavier raced in and, quite out of breath,
Said he was sure he would run to death.
He knew he just couldn't be absent or late
Or cause all the others to linger or wait.

Yancie bounced in and told the bugs, "Hey!"
Only one more to go.
They were well on their way
To getting together and showing that they
Could be of importance in everyone's day.

Zelda came in, and she looked mighty fine
As she made her way down
to the end of the line.
The twenty-six members
stood proud on their rugs,
For they formed the group called...

The

Aa
Bb
Cc
Dd

Ee
Ff
Gg

Hh
Ii
Jj

Kk
Ll
Mm

ALPHABUGS!

Nn

Oo

Pp

Qq

Rr

Ss

Tt

Uu

Vv

Ww

Xx

Yy

Zz

The

www.ingramcontent.com/pod-product-compliance
Lightning Source LLC
Chambersburg PA
CBHW042110040426
42448CB00002B/214